I0002167

Contents

Traffic Control Classifier Program   93

Program Array   103

Oxidize eBPF: eBPF programming with Rust

Introduction

The eBPF (extended Berkeley Packet Filter) infrastructure for Linux provides a **virtual machine (VM)** that can run programs safely inside the Linux kernel. These programs either modify the kernel behavior or safely exchange data between the kernel and the user space. The eBPF programs are event-driven and are run when the kernel or an application passes specific hook points. The hooks are predefined and include network events, system calls, function entry and exit, kernel tracepoints, and several others.

The eBPF infrastructure consists of the following parts.

Component	Location	Functionality
Compiler	Userspace	Convert eBPF program to bytecode
bpf syscall	Kernel	Load eBPF bytecode into the kernel
Verifier	Kernel	Ensure the program safety
JIT (Just In Time) compiler	Kernel	Convert bytecode to machine instructions

Component	Location	Functionality
VM (Virtual Machine)	Kernel	Run the eBPF program

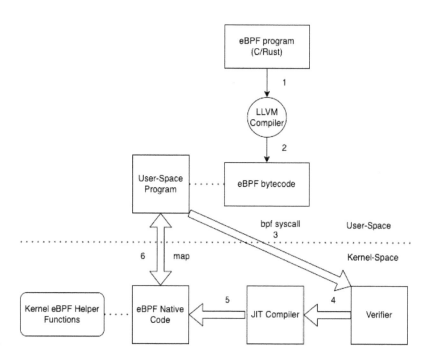

The eBPF program is usually written using a subset of high-level programming languages such as C or Rust and compiled to bytecode utilizing the LLVM compiler toolchain. A user space program loads the bytecode object into the kernel via the **bpf** system call. As part of loading the program in the kernel space, the eBPF verifier inside the kernel checks the validity of the bytecode before accepting it into the kernel. The verifier ensures that the eBPF program is safe to run and will terminate. Once all of the checks pass, the eBPF program is loaded into the kernel at the intended location in a kernel code path (hook), and it then waits for an appropriate event. When the event is received, the eBPF program is loaded, and the VM executes its bytecode. The eBPF infrastructure also includes an optional JIT compiler that converts eBPF byte-code to machine code, thereby enhancing the performance of the eBPF program by executing it directly using native instructions.

Data exchange between the kernel space and the user space is made possible using data structures called **maps**. The hook point to which an eBPF program can be attached and executed is determined by the **program type**. These concepts will be covered in detail in later chapters.

Part I

eBPF Virtual Machine

This chapter will go over the internals of the eBPF Virtual Machine (VM) with the help of an opensource **rbpf** project to illustrate how the VM executes an eBPF program. **rbpf** (https://github.com/qmonnet/rbpf) is the Rust implementation of the eBPF VM in the user space and provides a convenient way to try out the functionality of the eBPF VM in the user space. The workings of the VM will be illustrated by implementing a few sample programs using eBPF VM instructions. This chapter does not dwell on all of the details of the VM but provides enough context to understand how eBPF programs get executed in the Linux kernel.

Architecture

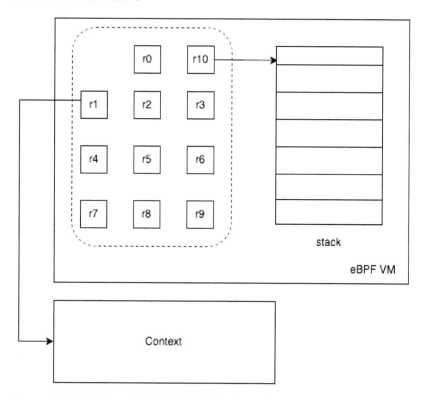

The eBPF VM is a 64-bit RISC (Reduced Instruction Set Computer) machine. The machine consists of 11 64-bit registers, a program counter (PC), and a 512-byte stack. Nine registers (r1 - r9) are general-purpose read-write registers, one register (r10) is a read-only stack-pointer, and the PC is implicit. The following table explains the functionality of each register.

Register	Functionality
r0	return value from function calls and exit value for eBPF programs

Register	Functionality
r1-r5	arguments for function calls. Upon program start, r1 contains the address of the input memory
r6-r9	callee saved registers that function calls will preserve
r10	read-only frame pointer to access stack

Each function call can have at most five arguments in registers r1-r5. This restriction applies to the eBPF program functions, ebpf-to-ebpf calls, and kernel helper function calls. Registers r1-r5 can only store numbers or pointers to the stack (to be used as arguments to functions), never direct pointers to arbitrary memory. All memory accesses must be done by first loading data to the eBPF stack before using it in the eBPF program. This restriction helps the eBPF verifier and simplifies the memory model to enable more straightforward correctness checking. When an eBPF program is started, the register r1 contains a pointer to the **context** memory, which serves as input data for the eBPF program to act upon.

Verifier

When an eBPF program is loaded into the Linux kernel using the **bpf** system call, before executing the program, it is first verified to make sure that it does not cause any ill side effects. This task is accomplished by running the eBPF program through a verifier. If the verification checks fail, the bpf system call returns -1 with an appropriate error set in **errno**.

The verification of an eBPF program is done using two steps.

- **Control Flow Analysis**: First, a DAG (Directed Acyclic Graph) of the eBPF instructions making up the program is generated, and this graph is traversed by the verifier using the DFS (Depth First Search) algorithm to ensure there are no loops, to prevent the eBPF programs from running forever. As part of walking the DAG, the verifier also ensures that there are no unused instructions (dead code) in the eBPF program and that the program has an expected end.

- **Data Flow Analysis**: The second check begins by starting at the first instruction and navigating all the possible code paths from it. The verifier monitors the registers and the stack while simulating all possible instruction executions and ensures that the program execution completes without causing any data-related issues, such as register or stack overflows.

Only when these checks pass is the eBPF program considered safe for execution. Please note the rbpf verifier does not perform any of these sophisticated checks.

Tail Calls

The eBPF VM limits the size of an eBPF program to restrict the problem size for the verification step. As of writing this book, the current limit is one million instructions. To overcome this limit on the eBPF program size, kernel functionality can be implemented by chaining multiple eBPF programs. An eBPF program can then call another eBPF program (eBPF-to-eBPF call) using a tail call (bpf_tail_call). As of writing this book, the tail call chain is limited to 32 calls.

Helper Functions

The eBPF VM architecture enables attaching of **helper functions** to the VM, which can then be directly called by the eBPF programs executed by the VM. This functionality will be demonstrated in the later part of the chapter.

Instruction Types

There are eight broad categories of instructions supported by the eBPF VM.

Type	Examples
LD	non-standard load operations
LDX	load into register operations
ST	store from immediate operations
STX	store from register operations
ALU32	32-bit arithmetic operations
ALU64	64-bit arithmetic operations
JMP32	32-bit jump operations
JMP64	64-bit jump operations

The following test programs will help illustrate how an eBPF program can be written using these instructions and executed on an eBPF VM.

Examples

Add two integer constants

```
extern crate rbpf;
use rbpf::helpers;
use rbpf::assembler::assemble;

#[test]
fn test_vm_add() {
  let prog = assemble("
      mov32 r0, 1
      mov32 r1, 2
      add r0, r1
      exit").unwrap();
  let vm = rbpf::EbpfVmNoData::new(Some(&prog))
          .unwrap();
  assert_eq!(vm.execute_program().unwrap(),
          0x3);
}
```

The **assemble** function takes an eBPF assembly program and converts it into eBPF bytecode. In the example above, we set the register **r0** to an immediate value of 1 and register **r1** to an immediate value of 2. The value of register r1 is then added to r0 to get a value of 3, which is verified by the assertion.

Add two integers stored in the context memory

Let us provide the two 32-bit integers as input to the VM using the context memory.

```
#[test]
```

```
fn test_vm_add_context() {
  let prog = assemble("
      ldxw  r0, [r1]
      ldxw  r1, [r1+4]
      add r0, r1
      be32 r0
      exit").unwrap();
  let mem = &mut [
      0x0, 0x22, 0x0, 0x0,
      0x0, 0x0, 0x33, 0x0
  ];
  let vm = rbpf::EbpfVmRaw::new(Some(&prog))
            .unwrap();
  assert_eq!(vm.execute_program(mem).unwrap(),
            0x00223300);
}
```

In this example, the eBPF program loads two 4-byte integers
to be added from the context memory. The **ldxw** instruction
reads 4 bytes from memory pointed to by **r1** and stores it
in register **r0**. The program loads the next 4 bytes from the
context memory into register **r1**. The add instruction adds
the integer value stored in r1 to the integer value stored in
r0. Finally, the result stored in r0 is converted to big-endian
format to ease the comparison in the assert statement.

Calculate Fibonacci Number

```
#[allow(unused_variables)]
pub fn fib(r1: u64, r2: u64, r3: u64,
    r4: u64, r5: u64) -> u64 {

    let mut i = 1;
```

```
    let mut j = 1;
    let mut k = r1;

    while k - 2 > 0 {
        j = i + j;
        i = j - i;
        k -= 1;
    }
    j
}

#[test]
fn test_vm_fib() {

    let prog = assemble("
        mov r2, r1
        ldxw r1,[r1]
        call 0
        stxw [r2+4], r0
        exit").unwrap();

    let mem = &mut [
        0xa, 0x0, 0x0, 0x0,
        0x0, 0x0, 0x0, 0x0
    ];
    let mut vm = rbpf::EbpfVmRaw::new(Some(&prog))
                    .unwrap();
    vm.register_helper(0, fib).unwrap();
    assert_eq!(vm.execute_program(mem).unwrap(),
            0x37);
    assert_eq!(mem[4], 0x37);
}
```

This example illustrates how the Fibonacci number can be

computed using the eBPF VM. **fib** is a Rust function that calculates the *nth* Fibonacci number. The function takes five input parameters that map to registers r1-r5. Of the five parameters, only the first parameter is used. The fib function is registered as a helper function with the eBPF VM with id 0. The eBPF program loads the value of n, which is located as a 32-bit integer in the first four bytes of the context memory. The function then computes the Fibonacci number by calling the registered helper function. It stores the result in register r0 and writes it to a 32-bit integer starting at offset 4 in the context memory using the **stxw** instruction.

The above programs assemble a BPF program into bytecode and then run the bytecode using the rbpf VM. It is also possible to JIT compile the program on an x86_64 platform and run it natively.

```
// Here prog is BPF program byte code
let mut vm = rbpf::EbpfVmRaw::new(prog)
                .unwrap();

// JIT-compile the program.
vm.jit_compile().unwrap();

// Then we execute it.
unsafe { vm.execute_program_jit()
            .unwrap(); }
```

Note that for rbpf, if errors occur during the program execution, the JIT-compiled version does not handle it as well as the interpreter, and the program may crash. For this reason, the functions are marked as unsafe.

JIT Compilation (Optional)

Suppose the Linux kernel hosting the eBPF program is compiled with the **CONFIG_BPF_JIT** option. In that case, the eBPF program bytecode is JIT (Just In Time) compiled into native assembly instructions after it has been verified and loaded. Otherwise, when the program is executed, it is run in the eBPF VM, which decodes and executes the eBPF bytecode instructions. The JIT compilation process offers execution performance near natively compiled in-kernel code.

Maps

An eBPF application consists of a user space program and the eBPF binary loaded by the user space program into the Linux kernel using the **bpf** system call. Maps are the message-passing mechanism between the user space program and the eBPF program executed by the eBPF VM in the kernel space. A map is a HashMap/HashTable data structure with a fixed-sized key and values. The type for the key and value of the map must be specified when a map is created. The key and the value are treated as binary blobs, and the user can store any data.

Overview

The aya-rs crate completely abstracts away the complexity of the eBPF map lifecycle, and the eBPF map functionality is very close to that of regular Rust data structures in the eBPF code.

User Space

An eBPF map can be declared in a user space program as follows.

```
// Userspace

use aya::maps::HashMap;
use std::net::Ipv4Addr;

...

let mut blocked_ips: HashMap<_, u32, u8> =
  HashMap::try_from(bpf.map_mut("BLOCKED_IPS")?)?;

let mut blocked_ip = Ipv4Addr::new(192, 168, 0, 1);
blocked_ips.insert(u32::from(blocked_ip), 1, 0)?;

blocked_ip = Ipv4Addr::new(192, 168, 0, 2);
blocked_ips.insert(u32::from(blocked_ip), 1, 0)?;
```

The above code creates a simple map (of type Hash) with the IPv4 address (32-bit) as the key and a flag (8-bit) as the value. This HashMap can be used as a Set data structure to communicate to the eBPF firewall program about which IP traffic needs to be blocked. In the above example, the IP addresses 192.168.0.1 and 192.168.0.2 were added to the map for the kernel eBPF firewall program to block them.

Kernel Space

The eBPF program in the kernel space can then access the hashmap.

```
// eBPF Program (Kernel)
use aya_bpf::{macros::{map}, maps::HashMap};
```

```
....

// Creates the map in the kernel
#[map(name = "BLOCKED_IPS")]
static mut BLOCKED_IPS: HashMap<u32, u8> =
    HashMap::<u32, u8>::with_max_entries(1024, 0);

....

if unsafe {BLOCKED_IPS.get(&src_addr).is_some()} {
    return Ok(xdp_action::XDP_DROP);
}
```

Note the string **BLOCKED_IPS** is used to tie a map between the userspace and the eBPF program.

Map Types

eBPF offers several different types of maps, and these types are defined in the **bpf_map_type** enum in the Linux kernel source code. The aya-rs crate has added support for a subset of them. The following sections provide information about the different map types implemented by the aya-rs crate.

Hash Map

This map resembles a HashTable/HashMap, and its use was covered in the overview section of this chapter.

Array Map

This map resembles an array. All array elements are pre-allocated and zero-initialized at init time. The size of the array is defined in the eBPF program using the bpf_map_def:: max_entries field.

```rust
// User space program

use aya::maps::Array;

...

let mut array: Array<_, u32> =
    Array::try_from(bpf.map_mut("ARRAY").unwrap())?;
...

// After the eBPF program has been loaded
array.set(1, 42, 0)?;
```

```rust
// eBPF Program (Kernel)

use aya_bpf::{macros::map, maps::Array};

...

#[map(name = "ARRAY")]
static mut array: Array<u32> =
    Array::with_max_entries(1024, 0);

...
```

```
let val = array.get(&1, 0)?;
assert_eq!(val, 42);
```

The above code defines a 32-bit unsigned integer array of size 1024 elements in the eBPF program. The program has an assertion to make sure the value added by the user space program is reflected in the kernel eBPF program.

Per-CPU Hash Map

This type of map is a specialized version of the regular Hash Map. When this type of map is allocated, each CPU sees its isolated version of the map, which makes it much more efficient for high-performant lookups and aggregations.

Per-CPU Array Map

This type of map is a specialized version of the regular Array Map. When this type of map is allocated, each CPU sees its isolated version of the map, which makes it much more efficient for high-performant lookups and aggregations.

Perf Event Array Map

This map stores **perf_events** data in a real-time buffer ring that communicates between the BPF program and the userspace programs. These maps are designed to forward the events that the kernel's tracing tools emit to user space programs for further processing. This is one of the most interesting maps and is the base of many observability tools.

For example, we would like to log the source and destination addresses of all the IPv4 packets. To do this, we first need to define a C-based struct to hold information about each event.

```
#[repr(C)]
pub struct PacketLog {
    pub src_addr: u32,
    pub dst_addr: u32,
}
```

```
// eBPF program
use aya_bpf::{macros::map, maps::PerfEventArray};

#[map(name = "EVENTS")]
static mut EVENTS: PerfEventArray<PacketLog> =
    PerfEventArray::<PacketLog>::with_max_entries(1024,
        0);
...

let source = u32::from_be(*ptr_at(&ctx,
  ETH_HDR_LEN + offset_of!(iphdr, saddr))?);

let dst = u32::from_be(*ptr_at(&ctx,
  ETH_HDR_LEN + offset_of!(iphdr, daddr))?);

let log_entry = PacketLog {
  src_addr: source,
  dst_addr: dst
};
EVENTS.output(&ctx, &log_entry, 0);
...
```

The user space program can then read these events from the
perf event array, as shown below.

```
// Userspace

use aya::maps::perf::AsyncPerfEventArray;

...
let mut perf_array =
  AsyncPerfEventArray::try_from(
      bpf.map_mut("EVENTS")?)?;

 loop {
  let events = buf.read_events(&mut buffers).await.
     unwrap();
  for i in 0..events.read {
    let buf = &mut buffers[i];
    let ptr = buf.as_ptr() as *const PacketLog;
    let data = unsafe { ptr.read_unaligned() };
    let src_addr = net::Ipv4Addr::from(data.src_addr);
    let dst_addr = net::Ipv4Addr::from(data.dst_addr);
    println!("LOG: SRC {} DST: {}"
      src_addr, dst_addr);
    }
  }
```

Stack

A stack map represents a LIFO (Last In, First Out) data structure.

```
// Userspace

use aya::maps::Stack;
```

```
...

let mut stack: Stack<_, u32> =
    Stack::try_from(bpf.map_mut("STACK").unwrap())?;

...


// After the eBPF program has been loaded
let addr = stack.pop(0)?;
```

```
// eBPF program

use aya_bpf::{macros::map, maps::Array};

...

#[map(name = "STACK")]
static mut stack: Stack<u32> =
    Stack::with_max_entries(1024, 0);

...

let mut addr:u32;

...
unsafe { STACK.push(&addr, 0).unwrap() };
```

Queue

Queue map represents a FIFO (First In, First Out) data structure. The API for this map is the same as that of the Stack

Map, except the **pop** function pops the first element instead of the last element added to the map.

LPM Trie

LPM (Longest Prefix Match) Trie is a data structure that uses the LPM algorithm to look up elements in the map. The LPM algorithm selects the element in a tree that matches with the longest lookup key from any other match in the tree. This algorithm is used in routers and other devices that keep traffic forwarding tables to check IP addresses.

```rust
// Userspace
use aya::maps::lpm_trie::{LpmTrie, Key};
...

let mut routes: LpmTrie<_, u32, u8> =
    LpmTrie::try_from(bpf.map_mut("ROUTES")?)?;

let route_1 =
  Key::new(u32::from(Ipv4Addr::new(10,0,0,0)),8);

routes.insert(&route_1, 1, 0)?;

let route_2 =
  Key::new(u32::from(Ipv4Addr::new(10,11,0,0)),16);

routes.insert(&route_2, 2, 0)?;
```

In this example, a user space program uses the LPM trie to store information about routes for two different subnets.

```rust
// eBPF program
```

```
use aya_bpf::maps::lpm_trie::{LpmTrie, Key};

#[map(name = "ROUTES")]
static mut routes: LpmTrie<u32, u8> =
  LpmTrie::with_max_entries(1024, 0);


...


let route = unsafe { routes.get(&dst_ip) };
```

The eBPF uses the routing information stored by the user space program to determine the route for the IP packet.

Socket Map/Hash

Sockmap and SockHash are maps used to store kernel-opened sockets. Sockmap is backed by an array and enforces keys to be four bytes. This works well for many use cases. However, this has become limiting in more prominent use cases where a Sockhash is more appropriate since it enables looking up the socket using the 5-tuple (protocol, source IP, source port, destination IP, destination port) lookup key.

Program Array Map

The eBPF verifier limits the number of eBPF instructions that can make up an eBPF program. To overcome this limit, a kernel functionality implemented using eBPF can be split into multiple eBPF programs (a maximum of 32 eBPF programs can be chained together). The program array map (BPF_MAP_TYPE_PROG_ARRAY) enables the control to jump from one eBPF program to another using the **bpf_tail_call** helper function. The program array map will be explained in detail using an example in the book's second part.

Program Types

An eBPF program type determines

- The subsystem in the Linux kernel that the eBPF program is attached to.
- The in-kernel helper functions that the program can call.

- The object type of the argument (context) passed to the program.

The eBPF program types vary as per the Linux kernel version. To get the complete list of the eBPF program types supported by your Linux distribution, use the command bpftool feature (please refer to the tools chapter). Following are some of the most interesting eBPF program types.

Type	Functionality
BPF_PROG_TYPE_SOCKET_FILTER	A network packet filter
BPF_PROG_TYPE_KPROBE	Determine whether a kprobe should fire or not

Type	Functionality
BPF_PROG_TYPE_XDP	A network packet filter run from the device-driver receive path
BPF_PROG_TYPE_PERF_EVENT	Determine whether a perf event handler should fire or not
BPF_PROG_TYPE_CGROUP_SKB	Traffic control for cgroup processes
BPF_PROG_TYPE_CGROUP_SOCK	Cgroup process socket control
BPF_PROG_TYPE_CGROUP_DEVICE	Determine if a device operation should be permitted or not
BPF_PROG_TYPE_CGROUP_SOCK_ADDR	Useful to implement socket-based NAT (network address translation)
BPF_PROG_TYPE_SOCK_OPS	A program for setting socket parameters
BPF_PROG_TYPE_SK_SKB	A network packet filter for forwarding packets between sockets
BPF_PROG_TYPE_SK_MSG	Egress packet filter

The second part of the book with go through multiple eBPF Rust programs that will cover some of these program types.

Tools

bpftool

bpftool is a utility for inspecting eBPF programs and maps. It comes in handy while debugging eBPF programs. This tool is not installed by default on any Linux distribution and must be compiled and installed using the source code. The instructions to install the tool can be found at https://github.com/libbpf/bpftool

Feature Display

```
bpftool feature
```

The **feature** subcommand shows all of the eBPF features supported by the Linux system on which the command is run. This subcommand shows

- eBPF kernel features that have been enabled
- Supported eBPF program types
- Kernel helper functions available for each eBPF program type

- Supported eBPF map types

A subset of the command output is shown below

```
Scanning system configuration...
bpf() syscall restricted to privileged users (admin can
    change)
JIT compiler is enabled
JIT compiler hardening is disabled
JIT compiler kallsyms exports are enabled for root
Global memory limit for JIT compiler for unprivileged
    users is 264241152 bytes
CONFIG_BPF is set to y
CONFIG_BPF_SYSCALL is set to y
CONFIG_HAVE_EBPF_JIT is set to y
CONFIG_BPF_JIT is set to y
CONFIG_BPF_JIT_ALWAYS_ON is set to y


...


Scanning system call availability...
bpf() syscall is available

Scanning eBPF program types...
eBPF program_type socket_filter is available
eBPF program_type kprobe is available
eBPF program_type sched_cls is available
eBPF program_type sched_act is available
eBPF program_type tracepoint is available
eBPF program_type xdp is available
eBPF program_type perf_event is available


...
```

```
Scanning eBPF map types...
eBPF map_type hash is available
eBPF map_type array is available
eBPF map_type prog_array is available


...


Scanning eBPF helper functions...
eBPF helpers supported for program type socket_filter:
            - bpf_map_lookup_elem
            - bpf_map_update_elem
            - bpf_map_delete_elem
            - bpf_ktime_get_ns
            - bpf_get_prandom_u32
...
```

Program Display

```
bpftool prog show
```

This command shows the currently loaded eBPF programs on
a Linux system. A sample output of the his command is shown
below

```
7: cgroup_skb   tag 6deef7357e7b4530   gpl
     loaded_at 2022-10-26T01:46:51+0000   uid 0
     xlated 64B   jited 55B   memlock 4096B
8: cgroup_skb   tag 6deef7357e7b4530   gpl
     loaded_at 2022-10-26T01:46:51+0000   uid 0
     xlated 64B   jited 55B   memlock 4096B
833: xdp   name firewall   tag 06a851c5a3c5d24c   gpl
```

```
loaded_at 2022-10-26T02:03:28+0000   uid 0
xlated 224B   jited 130B   memlock 4096B   map_ids 94
```

The numbers in the leftmost column are the ids of the eBPF programs. An individual program can be inspected using its id as follows.

```
bpftool prog show id 833

833: xdp   name firewall   tag 06a851c5a3c5d24c   gpl
     loaded_at 2022-10-26T02:03:28+0000   uid 0
     xlated 224B   jited 130B   memlock 4096B   map_ids 94
```

The above output can be printed in json format using the **-json** option

```
bpftool prog show id 833 —json

{"id":833,"type":"xdp","name":"firewall",
"tag":"06a851c5a3c5d24c","gpl_compatible":true,
"loaded_at":1666749808,"uid":0,"bytes_xlated":224,
"jited":true,"bytes_jited":130,
"bytes_memlock":4096,"map_ids":[94]}
```

This tool can also dump the raw eBPF instructions of an eBPF program as follows.

```
bpftool prog dump xlated id 833

   0: (b7) r0 = 0
   1: (79) r2 = *(u64 *)(r1 +8)
```

```
 2: (79) r1 = *(u64 *)(r1 +0)
 3: (bf) r3 = r1
 4: (07) r3 += 14
 5: (2d) if r3 > r2 goto pc+21
 6: (b7) r0 = 2
 7: (69) r3 = *(u16 *)(r1 +12)
 8: (55) if r3 != 0x8 goto pc+18
 9: (bf) r3 = r1
10: (07) r3 += 34
11: (b7) r0 = 0
12: (2d) if r3 > r2 goto pc+14
13: (61) r1 = *(u32 *)(r1 +26)
14: (dc) r1 = be32 r1
15: (63) *(u32 *)(r10 −4) = r1
16: (bf) r2 = r10
17: (07) r2 += −4
18: (18) r1 = map[id:94]
20: (85) call __htab_map_lookup_elem#199552
21: (15) if r0 == 0x0 goto pc+1
22: (07) r0 += 56
23: (bf) r1 = r0
24: (b7) r0 = 2
25: (15) if r1 == 0x0 goto pc+1
26: (b7) r0 = 1
27: (95) exit
```

Map Display

```
bpftool map show
```

This command shows information about eBPF maps loaded on
a Linux system. A sample output of the command is shown

below.

```
94: hash   name BLOCKED_IPS   flags 0x0
       key 4B   value 1B   max_entries 1024   memlock 8192B
```

The number on the left is the id of the map, and it can be used to view the map's contents as follows.

```
bpftool map dump id 94

key: 02 00 a8 c0   value: 01
key: 01 00 a8 c0   value: 01
Found 2 elements
```

In the above example, the two keys represent IP addresses (192.168.0.1 and 192.168.0.2) that need to be blocked by the eBPF firewall.

Unsafe Rust

For eBPF programs written using Rust, it is often required to access the Linux kernel data structures or call Linux kernel helper functions. **Unsafe Rust** is the glue that helps achieve this functionality. Following are the two essential functionalities enabled by unsafe Rust concerning eBPF programs.

- Ability to dereference a raw memory pointer that points to a Linux kernel data structure.
- Ability to call a Linux kernel helper function implemented in C.

Unsafe code in Rust is enclosed in a code block or a function block marked with the **unsafe** keyword. The best way to understand how unsafe Rust enables an eBPF program to interface with the Linux kernel is via the following two sample programs.

Kernel Data Structure Access

Every eBPF program gets called with a **context** passed as an input parameter. The context is a kernel data structure pointer; its type depends on the eBPF program type. The

memory referenced by the context can be accessed only with
unsafe Rust code.

```rust
// XDP eBPF program function

unsafe fn ptr_at<T>(ctx: &XdpContext, offset: usize)
    -> Result<*const T, ()> {

    let start = ctx.data();
    let end = ctx.data_end();
    let len = mem::size_of::<T>();

    if start + offset + len > end {
        return Err(());
    }

    Ok((start + offset) as *const T)
}
```

In the code snippet above, the **ptr_at** function is used by
an eBPF program of type BPF_PROG_TYPE_XDP. The function
takes ctx as an input parameter, a reference to an object of
type **XdpContext**. This reference represents a **C** struct variable of type **struct xdp_md** in the Linux kernel. The xdp_md
data structure points to a region in memory where a network
packet resides. The **start** and **end** variables store the starting and the ending memory addresses for the packet, while
the **offset** represents an offset within the packet. The ptr_at
function returns a pointer to a valid offset within the packet's
memory representation.

```rust
fn try_xdp_firewall(ctx: XdpContext) ->
        Result<u32, ()> {
```

```
let eth_type = u16::from_be(unsafe {
    *ptr_at(&ctx, offset_of!(ethhdr, h_proto))?

});
if eth_type != ETH_P_IP {
    return Ok(xdp_action::XDP_PASS);
}
let source = u32::from_be(unsafe {
    *ptr_at(&ctx, ETH_HDR_LEN + offset_of!(iphdr,
        saddr))?
});

if blocked_ip(source) {
  return Ok(xdp_action::XDP_DROP)
}
Ok(xdp_action::XDP_PASS)
}
```

The **try_xdp_firewall** uses the **ptr_at** function to get the **EtherType** from the raw packet. If the packet encapsulated in the ethernet frame is an IP packet, the source IP is extracted using the **ptr_at** function. If the source IP address is blocked, the packet is dropped by returning the XDP_DROP action.

Kernel Function Call

Unsafe Rust code also enables the calling of certain Linux kernel helper functions from the eBPF programs. The kernel helper functions that the eBPF program is permitted to call are contingent on the type of the program.

```
use aya_bpf::{
    programs::ProbeContext,
    helpers::bpf_ktime_get_ns,
};

fn try_nfs_file_read(ctx: ProbeContext)
         -> Result<u32, u32> {

  let start_mount_ns =
      unsafe { bpf_ktime_get_ns() };
  ....
  Ok(0)
}
```

In the code snippet above, **bpf_ktime_get_ns** is a Linux kernel helper function that returns the number of nanoseconds since boot time and is used to compute the time delta between events or as a timestamp. In this example, the bpf_ktime_get_ns function is called to record the start time of the NFS file read by encapsulating the helper function call in an **unsafe** block.

Part II

Hello World

This chapter will implement a fully working boilerplate eBPF program in Rust. In addition, a user space program that loads the eBPF program into the kernel and communicates with the eBPF program will be implemented in Rust. This chapter will walk you through both programs in detail and lay down the groundwork for the following chapters.

These programs will be implemented with the help of the aya-rs library. Aya-rs is a pure Rust library that uses the libc crate to execute the **bpf** syscall. It enables writing the eBPF programs in Rust, which are compiled to eBPF object code via the LLVM backend.

Setup

You will need to install Rust nightly toolchains on your Linux system since the Rust compiler eBPF target is currently tier-3 and has not stabilized as of the writing of this book.

```
rustup toolchain install nightly \
    —component rust—src
```

Once you have the Rust toolchains installed, you must also install bpf-linker

```
cargo install bpf-linker
```

To generate the scaffolding for your project, you're going to need **cargo-generate**, which you can install with

```
cargo install cargo-generate
```

Starting a new project

This chapter will create an eBPF program that will trace the **execve** system call.

Use the following command to generate a new eBPF project.

```
cargo generate https://github.com/aya-rs/aya-template

>    Project Name : tracepoint-demo
>    Destination: /home/vagrant/tmp/tracepoint-demo ...
>    Generating template ...
>    Which type of eBPF program?
   kprobe
   kretprobe
   fentry
   fexit
   uprobe
   uretprobe
   sock_ops
   socket_filter
```

```
    sk_msg
    xdp
    classifier
    cgroup_skb
    cgroup_sysctl
    cgroup_sockopt
>   tracepoint
    lsm
    tp_btf
>      Which tracepoint name? : sys_enter_execve
>      Which tracepoint category? : syscalls
```

Once the above commands are complete, your directory tree
should look like the following.

```
|-- Cargo.lock
|-- Cargo.toml
|-- README.md
|-- tracepoint-demo
|   |-- Cargo.toml
|   `-- src
|       `-- main.rs
|-- tracepoint-demo-common
|   |-- Cargo.toml
|   `-- src
|       `-- lib.rs
|-- tracepoint-demo-ebpf
|   |-- Cargo.lock
|   |-- Cargo.toml
|   |-- rust-toolchain.toml
|   `-- src
|       `-- main.rs
`-- xtask
    |-- Cargo.toml
```

```
`-- src
    |-- build_ebpf.rs
    |-- main.rs
    `-- run.rs
```

This directory structure contains the following three subdirectories

- **tracepoint-demo** contains the user-space program
- **tracepoint-demo-ebpf** contains the eBPF program
- **tracepoint-demo-common** contains the code for data structures and data types common to both user space and eBPF programs

Build

The user space program can be built using

```
cargo build
```

The eBPF program can be built using

```
cargo xtask build-ebpf
```

The release version of the eBPF program can be built using.

```
cargo xtask build-ebpf —release
```

Run

The userspace program, which loads the eBPF program into the kernel, can be run using.

```
cargo xtask run
```

On running the above command, the following output will be printed on the stdout output by the user space program.

```
02:45:45 [INFO] tracepoint_demo:
  [tracepoint-demo/src/main.rs:51] Waiting for Ctrl-C...
02:45:46 [INFO] tracepoint_demo:
  [src/main.rs:20] tracepoint sys_enter_execve called
02:45:46 [INFO] tracepoint_demo:
  [src/main.rs:20] tracepoint sys_enter_execve called
02:45:46 [INFO] tracepoint_demo:
  [src/main.rs:20] tracepoint sys_enter_execve called
02:45:46 [INFO] tracepoint_demo:
  [src/main.rs:20] tracepoint sys_enter_execve called
02:45:46 [INFO] tracepoint_demo:
  [src/main.rs:20] tracepoint sys_enter_execve called
02:45:46 [INFO] tracepoint_demo:
  [src/main.rs:20] tracepoint sys_enter_execve called
```

The above project creates a simple eBPF program attached to a **sys_enter_execve** tracepoint in the Linux kernel and is executed for each **sys_execve** syscall. The eBPF program on execution logs a perf event, and this event is returned to the user space for printing via the perf event array map. Exporting the logs from the kernel to the user space is abstracted from the developer and handled by the aya-log logging library.

eBPF program

```rust
1  #![no_std]
2  #![no_main]
3
4  use aya_bpf::{
5      macros::tracepoint,
6      programs::TracePointContext,
7  };
8  use aya_log_ebpf::info;
9
10 #[tracepoint(name = "tracepoint_demo")]
11 pub fn tracepoint_demo(ctx: TracePointContext)
12     -> u32 {
13
14     match try_tracepoint_demo(ctx) {
15         Ok(ret) => ret,
16         Err(ret) => ret,
17     }
18 }
19
20 fn try_tracepoint_demo(
21     ctx: TracePointContext,
22 ) -> Result<u32, u32> {
23     info!(&ctx, "sys_enter_execve called");
24     Ok(0)
25 }
26
27 #[panic_handler]
28 fn panic(_info: &core::panic::PanicInfo) -> ! {
29     unsafe { core::hint::unreachable_unchecked() }
30 }
```

In the above program, the function at line 11 is the entry point for the eBPF program. The core of the functionality is implemented by the **try_tracepoint_demo** function at line 20. This function takes the ctx (context) as an input which is a pointer to a kernel data structure. The structure of the context data can be figured out using.

```
cat /sys/kernel/debug/tracing/events/
    syscalls/sys_enter_execve/format
```

The **try_tracepoint_demo** logs a statement to the perf event array map using the **info!** macro which is then read by the user space program and printed on the console.

Userspace program

```
 1 use aya::programs::TracePoint;
 2 use aya::{include_bytes_aligned, Bpf};
 3 use aya_log::BpfLogger;
 4 use clap::Parser;
 5 use log::{info, warn};
 6 use tokio::signal;
 7 use simplelog::{
 8   ColorChoice, ConfigBuilder, LevelFilter,
 9   TermLogger, TerminalMode,
10 };
11
12 #[derive(Debug, Parser)]
13 struct Opt {}
14
15 #[tokio::main]
```

```rust
16 async fn main() -> Result<(), anyhow::Error> {
17   let opt = Opt::parse();
18
19   TermLogger::init(
20       LevelFilter::Debug,
21       ConfigBuilder::new()
22           .set_target_level(LevelFilter::Error)
23           .set_location_level(LevelFilter::Error)
24           .build(),
25       TerminalMode::Mixed,
26       ColorChoice::Auto,
27   )?;
28
29   #[cfg(debug_assertions)]
30   let mut bpf = Bpf::load(include_bytes_aligned!(
31       "../../target/bpfel-unknown-none/debug/
   tracepoint-demo"
32   ))?;
33
34   #[cfg(not(debug_assertions))]
35   let mut bpf = Bpf::load(include_bytes_aligned!(
36       "../../target/bpfel-unknown-none/release/
   tracepoint-demo"
37   ))?;
38   if let Err(e) = BpfLogger::init(&mut bpf) {
39       warn!(
40           "failed to initialize eBPF logger: {}",
41           e
42       );
43   }
44   let program: &mut TracePoint = bpf
45       .program_mut("tracepoint_demo")
46       .unwrap()
47       .try_into()?;
48   program.load()?;
```

```
49    program.attach("syscalls", "sys_enter_execve")?;
50
51    info!("Waiting for Ctrl-C...");
52    signal::ctrl_c().await?;
53    info!("Exiting...");
54
55    Ok(())
56 }
```

- Lines 19-27 initialize the logging library. The userspace program uses the simplelog crate to log the kernel events to the stdout.

- Lines 29-37: Load the contents of the binary eBPF program. Depending on the compile time configuration (cfg), the debug or release version of the eBPF program contents are loaded.

- Lines 38-43: Initialize the eBPF perf event array map for logging.

- Lines 44-49: Load the eBPF binary program into the kernel and attach it to **sys_enter_execve** tracepoint in the kernel.

- Lines 51-53: The program continues to run and output the execve logs to the console until it is terminated by the user using Ctrl-C.

Once the user terminates the user space program, the OS unloads the eBPF program.

aya-tool

The eBPF programs often need to know the kernel data structure they access. For example, your eBPF program might need
a **sk_buff** struct to access the packet information. It is possible to map the C kernel struct to a Rust struct manually; however, this process is error-prone and time-consuming. This is
where **aya-tool** comes in. It generates the rust binding for
Kernel data structures.

The aya-tool can be installed using the command.

```
$ cargo install \
    —git https://github.com/aya-rs/aya \
    — aya-tool
```

Once installed, the Rust binding for the Kernel data structure
is generated as follows.

```
aya-tool generate sk_buff > \
    myapp-ebpf/src/vmlinux.rs
```

You can import the **vmlinux** Rust module in your Rust eBPF
program and use the struct defined in the module and the context to access the kernel data. The eBPF socket filter chapter
will cover an example of using the Rust bindings generated by
aya-tool.

Source Code

The source code for all of the programs covered in this book is available at

https://github.com/vishpat/oxidize-ebpf

Trace Programs

In this chapter, we will cover four types of eBPF trace programs.

- Kernel Probe (kprobe)
- Kernel Tracepoint
- User Space Probe (uprobe)
- User Space Tracepoint

Kernel Probe (KProbe)

Linux kernel probes enable you to attach eBPF programs to kernel functions to gather information or modify the function's behavior. This section will provide examples of both.

The available kernel probes on a Linux system can be found using.

```
cat /proc/kallsyms
```

Block Mount

This section will create an eBPF program attached to the **open_ctree** kprobe. The eBPF program will modify the behavior of the function such that it will return ENOMEM instead of executing the body of the function. As a result, the **open_ctree** program will always fail with the attached eBPF program. The open_ctree function is executed while mounting a btrfs filesystem. So when this eBPF program is running, it prevents anyone from mounting the btrfs filesystem on the Linux system.

```
// userspace program

18 let mut bpf = Bpf::load(include_bytes_aligned!(
19     "../../target/bpfel-unknown-none/debug/block-
   mount"
20 ))?;
...
32 let program: &mut KProbe = bpf
33     .program_mut("block_mount")
34     .unwrap()
35     .try_into()?;
36 program.load()?;
37 program.attach("open_ctree", 0)?;
```

- Lines 18 - 20: Loads the eBPF program binary

- Lines 32 - 37: Loads the eBPF program into the kernel and attaches it to open_ctree kprobe.

```
// eBPF program
```

58

```
 1 #![no_std]
 2 #![no_main]
 3
 4 use aya_bpf::{
 5   helpers::bpf_override_return,
     macros::kprobe,
 6   programs::ProbeContext,
 7 };
 8 use aya_log_ebpf::info;
 9
10 const ENOMEM: i32 = -12;
11 #[kprobe(name = "block_mount")]
12 pub fn block_mount(ctx: ProbeContext) -> u32 {
13   match try_block_mount(ctx) {
14     Ok(ret) => ret,
15     Err(ret) => ret,
16   }
17 }
18
19 fn try_block_mount(
20     ctx: ProbeContext,
21 ) -> Result<u32, u32> {
22   info!(&ctx, "function open_ctree called");
23   unsafe {
24     bpf_override_return(ctx.regs,
25                         ENOMEM as u64)
26   };
27   Ok(0)
28 }
```

- Lines 19 - 28: The **try_block_mount** function is called at the start of the **open_ctree** function call. The eBPF helper function **bpf_override_return** short circuits the **open_ctree** function execution by returning ENOMEM.

This prevents the btrfs volume from being mounted.

File Access

This section will create an eBPF program and attach it to the **vfs_open** kernel function. The vfs_open kernel function is called whenever a Linux process opens a file. The eBPF program will be used to gather information about the file being opened. This information will be collected for non-root owned files and relayed to the userspace program using a perf event array map.

The file open event structure will be defined in a common library shared between userspace and the eBPF program.

```
#[repr(C)]
#[derive(Clone, Copy, Debug)]
pub struct FileData {
    pub pid: c_uint,
    pub pgid: c_uint,
    pub uid: c_uint,
    pub d_parent: [c_uchar; 32usize],
    pub name: [c_uchar; 32usize],
}
```

The userspace program is implemented using the tokio runtime to extract events from the perf event array map and output the information to the stdout.

```
// userspace program
52 let program: &mut KProbe = bpf
53     .program_mut("kernel_probe")
54     .unwrap()
```

60

```
55      .try_into()?;
56 program.load()?;
57 program.attach("vfs_open", 0)?;
58
59 let mut perf_array =
60     AsyncPerfEventArray::try_from(
61         bpf.map_mut("EVENTS")?,
62     )?;
63 for cpu_id in online_cpus()? {
64  let mut buf = perf_array.open(cpu_id, None)?;
65
66  task::spawn(async move {
67    let mut buffers = (0..10)
68        .map(|_| BytesMut::with_capacity(1024))
69        .collect::<Vec<_>>();
70    loop {
71        let events = buf
72            .read_events(&mut buffers)
73            .await
74            .unwrap();
75        for i in 0..events.read {
76          let buf = &mut buffers[i];
77          let ptr = buf.as_ptr()
78              as *const FileData;
79          let data = unsafe {
80              ptr.read_unaligned()
81          };
82          println!(
83            "file_data: pid: {}, pgid: {},
                uid: {}, path: {} ",
84            data.pid,
85            data.pgid,
86            data.uid,
87            format!(
88                "{}/{}",
```

```
89                      from_utf8(&data.d_parent).unwrap(),
90                      from_utf8(&data.name).unwrap()
91                  )
92              );
93          }
94      }
95  });
96 }
```

- Lines 52 - 57: Load the eBPF program into the kernel and attach it to the **vfs_probe** kernel function.

- Lines 59 - 62: Declare a perf event array map to store information about the file open events.

- Lines 66 - 96: Spawn a tokio task per CPU to gather file open events using the perf event array map.

The **vfs_open** Linux kernel function is passed the **path C struct** as its first parameter.

```
struct path {
    struct vfsmount *mnt;
    struct dentry *dentry;
};
```

The relevant file information is extracted using this struct and the eBPF helper functions to create the file open event. The event information is then added to the perf event array map.

```
// eBPF program
23 #[map(name = "EVENTS")]
24 static mut EVENTS: PerfEventArray<FileData> =
```

```
25   PerfEventArray::<FileData>::with_max_entries(
26       1024, 0,
27   );
....
37 unsafe fn try_kernel_probe(
38     ctx: ProbeContext,
39 ) -> Result<u32, u32> {
40   let path: *const path = ctx.arg(0)
41                             .ok_or(1u32)?;
42   let dentry: *const dentry =
43       bpf_probe_read(&(*path).dentry)
44           .map_err(|_| 1u32)?;
45   let inode: *const inode =
46       bpf_probe_read(&(*dentry).d_inode)
47           .map_err(|_| 1u32)?;
48   let k_uid: kuid_t =
49       bpf_probe_read(&(*inode).i_uid)
50           .map_err(|_| 1u32)?;
51   let i_uid: c_uint =
52       bpf_probe_read(&k_uid.val)
53           .map_err(|_| 1u32)?;
54   let d_iname: [c_uchar; 32usize] =
55       bpf_probe_read(&(*dentry).d_iname)
56           .map_err(|_| 1u32)?;
57   let d_parent: *const dentry =
58       bpf_probe_read(&(*dentry).d_parent)
59           .map_err(|_| 1u32)?;
60   let d_parent_name: [c_uchar; 32usize] =
61       bpf_probe_read(&(*d_parent).d_iname)
62           .map_err(|_| 1u32)?;
63   let pgid =
64     (bpf_get_current_pid_tgid() >> 32) as u32;
65   let pid = bpf_get_current_pid_tgid() as u32;
66
67   if i_uid == 0 {
```

```
68         return Ok(0);
69    }
70
71    let file_data = FileData {
72         pid: pid,
73         pgid: pgid,
74         uid: i_uid,
75         d_parent: d_parent_name,
76         name: d_iname,
77    };
78
79    EVENTS.output(&ctx, &file_data, 0);
80    Ok(0)
81 }
```

- Lines 23 - 27: Create the perf event array map.

- Lines 42 - 62: Get information about the file being opened.

- Lines 63 - 65: Get the PID (process id) and the PGID (process group id) of the process opening the file.

- Lines 71 - 77: Create the perf event and add it to the perf event array map.

Kernel Tracepoint

The kernel tracepoint eBPF program will be based on the **Hello World** program from the previous chapter. The **try_tracepoint_demo** function will be modified to access the context (kernel data structure) to extract the file name of the executed binary. In addition, the eBPF program will log the PID of the process.

64

As mentioned in the previous chapter, the **ctx** parameter refers to a kernel data structure. The details of this data structure can be inspected with

```
cat /sys/kernel/debug/tracing/
    events/syscalls/sys_enter_execve/format
name: sys_enter_execve
ID: 729
format:
  field:unsigned short common_type;
    offset:0;        size:2; signed:0;
  field:unsigned char common_flags;
    offset:2;        size:1; signed:0;
  field:unsigned char common_preempt_count;
    offset:3;        size:1; signed:0;
  field:int common_pid;    offset:4;
    size:4; signed:1;
  field:int __syscall_nr;  offset:8;
    size:4; signed:1;
  field:const char * filename;
    offset:16;       size:8; signed:0;
  field:const char *const * argv;
    offset:24;       size:8; signed:0;
  field:const char *const * envp;
    offset:32;       size:8; signed:0;
```

The above output shows that the **filename** parameter for the **sys_execve** system call is located at offset 16 inside the context.

The first step for the eBPF program to access the kernel information is to import eBPF helper functions. These functions enable an eBPF program to interact with the system or the context in which they work.

```
 2  #![no_main]
 3
 4  use aya_bpf::{
 5      cty::c_long,
 6      helpers::{
 7          bpf_get_current_pid_tgid,
 8          bpf_probe_read_user_str_bytes,
 9      },
10      macros::tracepoint,
11      programs::TracePointContext,
12  };
```

- Line 7: Helper function to get the process and thread group id of the process making the syscall. This function returns a 64-bit value of which the lower 32-bits contain the process id, and the upper 32-bits contain the thread group id.

- Line 8: Helper function to perform a **safe** copy of string bytes from a source to a destination. If the source buffer length exceeds the destination buffer, the copy is truncated to fit the destination buffer. The destination buffer is always NULL terminated. This function returns a slice of bytes up to and not including NULL.

```
16  #[tracepoint(name = "tracepoint_demo")]
17  pub fn tracepoint_demo(
18      ctx: TracePointContext,
19  ) -> c_long {
20      match try_tracepoint_demo(ctx) {
21          Ok(ret) => ret,
22          Err(ret) => ret,
```

```
23    }
24 }
25
26 fn try_tracepoint_demo(
27      ctx: TracePointContext,
28 ) -> Result<c_long, c_long> {
29
30    const FILENAME_OFFSET: usize = 16;
31    let filename_addr: u64 =
32        unsafe { ctx.read_at(FILENAME_OFFSET)? };
33
34    const BUF_SIZE: usize = 128;
35    let mut buf = [0u8; BUF_SIZE];
36    // read the filename
37    let filename = unsafe {
38        core::str::from_utf8_unchecked(
39            bpf_probe_read_user_str_bytes(
40                filename_addr as *const u8,
41                &mut buf,
42            )?
43        )
44    };
45
46
47    let pid = bpf_get_current_pid_tgid() as u32;
48
49    info!(&ctx, "{} {}", pid, filename);
50
51    Ok(0)
52 }
```

- Line 30: Defines the location of the filename offset.

- Lines 31 - 32: Get the memory address of the filename parameter.

- Lines 34 - 35: Declare a local variable to store the file-name.

- Lines 37 - 44: Return a UTF-8 encoded filename.

- Line 47: Get the PID of the process making the system call.

- Line 49: Log the PID and the filename.

User Space Probe (UProbe)

Userspace probes (UProbe) enable you to attach eBPF programs to functions run by the userspace programs. When you define an uprobe, the kernel creates a trap around the attached instruction. When your application reaches the instruction, the kernel triggers an event that executes the eBPF program.

As an example, we will create two eBPF programs that will be used in conjunction to calculate the time spent by process in the libc **sendfile** function. An eBPF map will be used to implement this functionality. The first eBPF program will be executed at the start of the **sendfile**, while the second eBPF program will be executed before the **sendfile** function returns.

```
47 let mut _counters: HashMap<_, u32, u64> =
48     HashMap::try_from(bpf.map_mut("SENDFILE")?)?;
49
50 let program: &mut UProbe = bpf
51     .program_mut("binary_probe")
52     .unwrap()
53     .try_into()?;
54 program.load()?;
```

```
55 program.attach(
56     Some("sendfile"),
57     0,
58     "libc",
59     opt.pid.try_into()?
60 )?;
61
62 let program: &mut UProbe = bpf
63     .program_mut("binary_retprobe")
64     .unwrap()
65     .try_into()?;
66 program.load()?;
67 program.attach(
68     Some("sendfile"),
69     0,
70     "libc",
71     opt.pid.try_into()?
72 )?;
```

Lines 47 - 48: Declares an eBPF map to store the PID as the key and the start timestamp as the value.

Lines 50 - 60: Loads an eBPF program and attaches it to the start of the **sendfile** function in the libc library.

Lines 62 - 72: Loads an eBPF program and attaches it to the end of the **sendfile** function in the libc library.

```
// eBPF program
13 #[map(name = "SENDFILE")]
14 static mut SENDFILE: HashMap<u32, u64> =
15     HashMap::<u32, u64>::with_max_entries(1024, 0);
16
17 #[uprobe(name = "binary_probe")]
18 pub fn binary_probe(ctx: ProbeContext)
```

```rust
    -> u32 {
19  match try_binary_probe(ctx) {
20    Ok(ret) => ret,
21    Err(ret) => ret,
22  }
23 }
24
25 fn try_binary_probe(
26     ctx: ProbeContext,
27 ) -> Result<u32, u32> {
28   info!(&ctx, "Sendfile function enter");
29   let pid = bpf_get_current_pid_tgid() as u32;
30   let current_time = unsafe { bpf_ktime_get_ns() };
31   unsafe {
32       SENDFILE
33           .insert(&pid, &current_time, 0)
34           .unwrap()
35   };
36   Ok(0)
37 }
38
39 #[uretprobe(name = "binary_retprobe")]
40 pub fn binary_retprobe(ctx: ProbeContext)
    -> u32 {
41   match try_binary_retprobe(ctx) {
42     Ok(ret) => ret,
43     Err(ret) => ret,
44   }
45 }
46
47 fn try_binary_retprobe(
48     ctx: ProbeContext,
49 ) -> Result<u32, u32> {
50   info!(&ctx, "Sendfile function return");
51   let pid = bpf_get_current_pid_tgid() as u32;
```

```
52    let start_time =
53        unsafe { SENDFILE.get(&pid).unwrap_or(&0) };
54    let end_time = unsafe { bpf_ktime_get_ns() };
55    let duration = end_time - start_time;
56    info!(
57        &ctx,
58        "Sendfile duration: for pid {} : {} nsecs",
59        pid,
60        duration
61    );
62    unsafe { SENDFILE.remove(&pid).unwrap() };
63    Ok(0)
64 }
```

Lines 13 - 15: Create an eBPF map to store the PID and start timestamp.

Lines 17 - 23: Create an eBPF program that will be executed at the start of the sendfile function.

Lines 25 - 37: Get the process id, the current timestamp and add an entry to the eBPF map.

Lines 39 - 45: Creates an eBPF program that will be executed just before the sendfile function returns.

Lines 47 - 64: Get the process id and, using the process id, get the start timestamp from the eBPF map. Using this value and the current timestamp (end_time), calculate the duration of the sendfile function and log the information.

User Space Tracepoint

Following is a sample C program with a static probe known as a User Statically-Defined Tracing (USDT) probe added to it. This type of probe provides a low-overhead way of instrumenting user-space code and a convenient way to debug applications running in production.

```
// The following code was obtained from
// https://lwn.net/Articles/753601/

#include <sys/sdt.h>
#include <sys/time.h>
#include <unistd.h>

int main(int argc, char **argv)
{
    struct timeval tv;

    while(1) {
        gettimeofday(&tv, NULL);
        DTRACE_PROBE1(test-app, test-probe,
                            tv.tv_sec);
        sleep(1);
    }
    return 0;
}
```

This simple program runs until interrupted. It fires a probe and then calls sleep() to wait for one second until the loop starts again. The DTRACE_PROBE() macro is used to create probe points at desired locations, in this case, immediately before sleeping. This macro takes a provider name, probe name, and arguments as parameters. There's a separate DTRACE_PROBEn() macro for each argument count. For example, if your probe has three arguments, you must use DTRACE_PROBE3().

It is possible to write a **user space** eBPF program that attaches to the DTrace probe and extracts the values of the arguments. However, support for user space tracepoints is not available in the **aya-rs** library as of the writing of this book.

Socket Filter Program

Socket Filter Programs were the first type of BPF programs that were added to the Linux kernel. When the eBPF program is attached to a raw socket, it gets access to all of the packets processed by the socket. eBPF socket filter programs cannot modify the packet's contents or change the packet's destination. These eBPF programs are mainly used for observability purposes only.

In this chapter, we will create a Socket Filter Program that will be used to count the number of UDP, TCP, and ICMP packets received by the Linux server.

Common lib

The following constants that map to the protocol numbers will be defined in the library common to the user space program and the eBPF.

```
pub const IP_PROTO: u16 = 0x0800;
pub const TCP_PROTO: u8 = 0x6;
pub const ICMP_PROTO: u8 = 0x1;
pub const UDP_PROTO: u8 = 0x11;
```

User Space Program

```
56 let mut counters: HashMap<_, u8, u32> =
57   HashMap::try_from(bpf.map_mut("COUNTERS")?)?;
58
59 let client = unsafe {
60   libc::socket(
61       libc::AF_PACKET,
62       libc::SOCK_RAW,
63       ETH_P_ALL.to_be() as i32,
64   )
65 };
66 let prog: &mut SocketFilter = bpf
67       .program_mut("packet_counter")
68       .unwrap()
69       .try_into()?;
70 prog.load()?;
71 prog.attach(client)?;
72
73 info!("Waiting for Ctrl-C...");
74 signal::ctrl_c().await?;
75 info!("Exiting...");
76 println!(
77   "TCP: {}",
78   counters.get(&TCP_PROTO, 0).unwrap_or(0)
79 );
80 println!(
81   "UDP: {}",
82   counters.get(&UDP_PROTO, 0).unwrap_or(0)
83 );
```

```
84 println!(
85   "ICMP: {}",
86   counters.get(&ICMP_PROTO, 0).unwrap_or(0)
87 );
```

Lines 56 - 57: Declares an eBPF map with an integer key that maps to the protocol and a value corresponding to the packet count.

Lines 59 - 65: Use the libc crate to create a raw socket. This raw socket can snoop on all the packets received by the Linux box.

Lines 66 - 71: Loads the Socket Filter eBPF Program into the kernel and attaches it to the raw socket. The eBPF program will be run each time the raw socket receives a packet.

Lines 73 - 75: Wait to receive Ctrl-C from the user.

Lines 76 - 87: Print the count of each type of packet received.

eBPF Program

```
14 use packet_counter_common::{
15   IP_PROTO, TCP_PROTO, UDP_PROTO,
16 };
17 use vmlinux::{ethhdr, iphdr};
18
19 const ETH_HDR_LEN: usize = mem::size_of::<ethhdr>();
20 const IP_HDR_LEN: usize = mem::size_of::<iphdr>();
21
22 #[map(name = "COUNTERS")]
23 static mut COUNTERS: HashMap<u8, u32> =
24   HashMap::<u8, u32>::with_max_entries(3, 0);
```

```
25
26 fn increment_counter(proto: u8) {
27    let mut counter =
28        unsafe { COUNTERS.get(&proto).unwrap_or(&0) };
29    let new_count = *counter + 1;
30    unsafe {
31        COUNTERS.insert(&proto, &new_count, 0).unwrap()
32    };
33 }
34
35 #[socket_filter(name = "packet_counter")]
36 pub fn packet_counter(_ctx: SkBuffContext) -> i64 {
37    let eth_proto = u16::from_be(
38        _ctx.load(offset_of!(ethhdr, h_proto))
39            .unwrap(),
40    );
41    let ip_proto = _ctx
42        .load::<u8>(
43            ETH_HDR_LEN +
44                offset_of!(iphdr, protocol),
44        )
45        .unwrap();
46
47    if eth_proto != IP_PROTO {
48        return 0;
49    }
50
51    match ip_proto {
52      TCP_PROTO => increment_counter(TCP_PROTO),
53      ICMP_PROTO => increment_counter(ICMP_PROTO),
54      UDP_PROTO => increment_counter(UDP_PROTO),
55      _ => {}
56    }
57
58    return 0;
```

```
59 }
```

Lines 14 - 16: Import constants from the common library.

Lines 17 - 20: Determine the Ethernet and IP header length using the Kernel structures defined in the **vmlinux** Rust module. The Rust module containing the bindings for the kernel data structures is generated using the aya-tool.

Lines 22 - 24: Define the eBPF map to store the protocol counter values.

Lines 26 - 33: Function to increment the counter value for a given protocol.

Lines 36: Defines a socket filter eBPF program that is provided the sk_buff structure as the context.

Lines 37 - 40: Get the EtherType from the packet.

Lines 41 - 45: Get the IP protocol from the packet.

Lines 55 - 56: Use the IP protocol to increment the counter.

Express Data Path Program

eXpress Data Path (XDP) is a safe, programmable, high-performance, kernel-integrated packet processor in the Linux network data path that can execute eBPF programs when the NIC driver receives a packet. This enables XDP programs to make decisions about the received packet (drop, modify or allow it) at the earliest possible time. XDP programs help determine the received packet's fate, modify its contents, or return a result code. The resulting code is used to determine what happens to the packet in the form of an action. Following are five XDP result codes and their corresponding actions

XDP Result Code	Action
XDP_DROP	Drop the packet

XDP Result Code	Action
XDP_TX	Forward the packet back out of the same NIC it arrived on. This can happen before or after the packet has been modified
XDP_REDIRECT	Same as XDP_TX, but the packet is routed through another NIC
XDP_PASS	Pass packet to normal network stack for processing
XDP_ABORTED	eBPF program error resulting in packet drop

One of the main benefits of XDP is that it allows you to perform tasks very early in the networking stack, before the kernel has fully processed the packet. This means that you can use XDP to perform certain operations on packets at a very high speed, with minimal overhead. This makes XDP particularly useful for high-performance networking applications, such as load balancing, intrusion detection, and traffic shaping.

In this chapter, we will implement a simple firewall using an eBPF XDP program. The user space program will provide the eBPF program with a list of blacklisted source IP addresses. The eBPF program will drop the packets using the XDP_DROP action for the traffic originating from these IP addresses.

User Space program

```
49 let mut blocked_ips: HashMap<_, u32, u8> =
50     HashMap::try_from(
51         bpf.map_mut("BLOCKED_IPS")?,
52     )?;
53 let mut blocked_ip = Ipv4Addr::new(192, 168, 0, 1);
54 blocked_ips.insert(u32::from(blocked_ip), 1, 0)?;
55
56 blocked_ip = Ipv4Addr::new(192, 168, 0, 2);
57 blocked_ips.insert(u32::from(blocked_ip), 1, 0)?;
58
59 let program: &mut Xdp = bpf
60     .program_mut("firewall")
61     .unwrap()
62     .try_into()?;
63 program.load()?;
64 program
65     .attach("eth0", XdpFlags::default())
66     .context("failed to attach the XDP program")?;
```

Lines 49 - 52: eBPF map for IP addresses whose traffic needs to be dropped.

Lines 53 - 57: Add IP addresses **192.168.0.1** and **192.168.0.2** to the eBPF map.

Lines 59 - 63: Load the eBPF XDP firewall program into the kernel.

Lines 64 - 66: Attach the eBPF program to an ethernet interface on which the packets are received.

eBPF program

```
15 use vmlinux::{ethhdr, iphdr};
16
17 pub const IP_PROTO: u16 = 0x0800;
18 pub const TCP_PROTO: u8 = 0x6;
19 const ETH_HDR_LEN: usize = mem::size_of::<ethhdr>();
20
21 #[map(name = "BLOCKED_IPS")]
22 static mut BLOCKED_IPS: HashMap<u32, u8> =
23     HashMap::<u32, u8>::with_max_entries(1024, 0);
24
25 #[xdp(name = "firewall")]
26 pub fn firewall(ctx: XdpContext) -> u32 {
27     match try_firewall(ctx) {
28         Ok(ret) => ret,
29         Err(_) => xdp_action::XDP_ABORTED,
30     }
31 }
32
33 unsafe fn ptr_at<T>(
34     ctx: &XdpContext,
35     offset: usize,
36 ) -> Result<*const T, ()> {
37     let start = ctx.data();
38     let end = ctx.data_end();
39     let len = mem::size_of::<T>();
40
41     if start + offset + len > end {
42         return Err(());
43     }
```

```
44      Ok((start + offset) as *const T)
45 }
46
47 fn try_firewall(ctx: XdpContext) -> Result<u32, u32>
   {
48      let start = ctx.data();
49      let end = ctx.data_end();
50
51      // Without the boundary check,
52      // the eBPF verification will fail
53      if start + ETH_HDR_LEN > end {
54          return Err(xdp_action::XDP_PASS);
55      }
56
57      let eth_proto = u16::from_be(unsafe {
58          *ptr_at(&ctx, offset_of!(ethhdr, h_proto))
59              .unwrap()
60      });
61      if eth_proto != IP_PROTO {
62          return Ok(xdp_action::XDP_PASS);
63      }
64
65      // Without the boundary check,
66      // the eBPF verification will fail
67      if start + ETH_HDR_LEN + mem::size_of::<iphdr>()
68          > end
69      {
70          return Err(xdp_action::XDP_PASS);
71      }
72
73      let src_addr = u32::from_be(unsafe {
74          *ptr_at(
75              &ctx,
76              ETH_HDR_LEN + offset_of!(iphdr, saddr),
77          )
```

```
78              .unwrap()
79          });
80          if unsafe { BLOCKED_IPS.get(&src_addr).is_some()
     }
81          {
82              return Ok(xdp_action::XDP_DROP);
83          }
84
85          Ok(xdp_action::XDP_PASS)
86 }
```

Line 15: Import Rust structs for the Ethernet and IP headers from the vmlinux Rust module. This Rust module is generated using the aya-tool.

Lines 21 - 23: Define an eBPF map to hold the source IP addresses whose traffic needs to be dropped.

Lines 25 - 31: The XDP firewall eBPF program.

Lines 33 - 45: A helper function that returns a pointer to a data type inside the context memory at a particular offset. The data type is determined by the generic type parameter **T**.

Line 48: Starting address of the context (packet) memory.

Line 49: Ending address of the context (packet) memory.

Lines 51 - 63: Get the EtherType for the packet. If the packet is not an IP packet, proceed with regular processing.

Lines 67 - 29: Get the source IPv4 address.

Lines 80 - 82: Drop the packet if the source IP address is in the block list.

Linux Security Module Program

Linux Security Modules (LSMs) are kernel security frameworks that provide a way to extend the kernel's security capabilities in a modular and flexible way. LSMs allow you to add custom security policies and enforcement mechanisms to the kernel to protect against various threats, such as malicious code, unauthorized access, and data tampering.

There are several different LSMs available for Linux, each with its own set of features and capabilities. Some common LSMs include AppArmor, SELinux, and Tomoyo. These LSMs provide different security policies and enforcement mechanisms and can be used to protect against different types of threats.

To use an LSM, you will need to configure the appropriate security policies and rules for your system. This can typically be done using configuration files or tools provided by the LSM. Once the policies are configured, the LSM will operate transparently in the background, enforcing the security policies as needed.

For example, suppose you want to use an LSM to prevent a

certain program from accessing certain files on your system. You could configure the LSM to deny access to these files for the program, and the LSM would enforce this policy by denying access to the files whenever the program tried to access them.

In general, LSMs are a powerful tool for enhancing the security of a Linux system. By configuring the appropriate security policies and rules, you can protect against a wide range of threats and ensure that the system is secure.

An LSM can be implemented as an eBPF program and be attached to an LSM Hook. LSM allows eBPF programs to mediate access to kernel objects by placing hooks in the kernel code just ahead of the access. Before the kernel accesses an internal object, a hook calls the eBPF program to determine if the access is permitted. The eBPF program can either let the access occur or deny access, forcing an error code return.

User Space Program

A list of the active security modules can be found as follows.

```
cat /sys/kernel/security/lsm
lockdown,capability,landlock,yama,apparmor,bpf
```

bpf present in the output ensures that the LSM can be implemented using eBPF.

In this section, we will implement an eBPF program that will block the execution of certain binary programs on the Linux machine. The list of the binary programs that need to be blocked will be passed to the eBPF program by the user space program using an eBPF map. The eBPF program will be attached to the **task_alloc** LSM hook to prevent a prohibited binary from running.

```
#[repr(C)]
#[derive(Clone, Copy)]
pub struct BinaryName {
    pub name: [u8; 16],
}
```

BinaryName struct is defined in the common library to hold the program name. This struct will be shared between the user space and the eBPF program.

```
3 use aya::{programs::Lsm, Btf};
...
49 let btf = Btf::from_sys_fs()?;
50 let program: &mut Lsm = bpf
51     .program_mut("task_alloc")
52     .unwrap()
53     .try_into()?;
54 info!("Loading task_alloc program");
55 program.load("task_alloc", &btf)?;
56 program.attach()?;
57
58 let mut blocklist: HashMap<_, BinaryName, u32> =
59    HashMap::try_from(bpf.map_mut("BLOCKLIST")?)?;
60
61 let progs = vec!["node", "apt"];
62
63 for prog in progs.iter() {
64    let mut binary_name: BinaryName =
65        BinaryName { name: [0; 16] };
```

```
66   binary_name.name[..prog.len()]
67       .copy_from_slice(&prog.as_bytes());
68   blocklist.insert(binary_name, 1, 1)?;
69 }
```

Line 49: Loads BTF (BPF Type Format) metadata from /sys/k-ernel/btf/vmlinux.

Lines 50 - 56: Load the eBPF program as LSM into the Linux kernel using the BTF metadata.

Lines 58 - 59: eBPF map containing the list of prohibited binary programs.

Lines 61 - 68: Initialize the eBPF map with the list of prohibited binary program names.

eBPF program

```
18 #[map(name = "BLOCKLIST")]
19 static mut BLOCKLIST: HashMap<BinaryName, u32> =
20   HashMap::<BinaryName, u32>::with_max_entries(
21        16, 0,
22   );
23
24 #[lsm(name = "task_alloc")]
25 pub fn task_alloc(ctx: LsmContext) -> i32 {
26   match try_task_alloc(ctx) {
27     Ok(ret) => ret,
28     Err(ret) => ret,
29   }
30 }
31
```

```
32 fn block_binary(binary_name: &BinaryName) -> bool {
33   unsafe { BLOCKLIST.get(binary_name).is_some() }
34 }
35
36 fn try_task_alloc(
37     ctx: LsmContext,
38 ) -> Result<i32, i32> {
39   let task: *const task_struct = unsafe {
40       ctx.arg::<*const task_struct>(0)
41           as *const task_struct
42   };
43
44   let name = unsafe { &(*task).comm };
45   let mut binary_name: BinaryName =
46       BinaryName { name: [0; 16] };
47
48   let mut i: usize = 0;
49   for c in name.iter() {
50       binary_name.name[i] = *c as u8;
51       i += 1;
52   }
53   let block = block_binary(&binary_name);
54   if block {
55       return Err(-1);
56   }
57
58   Ok(0)
59 }
```

- Lines 19 - 22: eBPF map to store prohibited binary program names.

- Lines 32 - 34: Check if the program binary is prohibited.

- Lines 39 - 42: The LSM hook for **task_alloc** receives the

task_struct as the first input parameter. A pointer to the task_struct is stored in the local **task** variable.

- Lines 44 - 51: Extract the program name of the task.

- Lines 53 - 55: Return an error if the binary program is prohibited. This will fail the task allocation process, and the program will be prevented from being able to run.

Traffic Control Classifier Program

Linux traffic control is a tool that can be used to identify packets of network traffic based on various criteria, such as the source and destination IP addresses, port numbers, and protocol. The traffic control can then assign these packets to different "classes" or categories based on the characteristics of the traffic.

eBPF allows you to attach custom programs to various points in the kernel's networking stack. One way eBPF can be used with a traffic control is to implement custom packet filtering rules. For example, you might want to use eBPF to identify packets that match certain criteria and pass them to a traffic control for further processing. Another way that eBPF can be used with a traffic control is to implement custom traffic shaping or queueing disciplines. For example, you might want to use eBPF to implement a custom queueing discipline that uses packet metadata (such as the source and destination IP addresses) to make decisions about how to prioritize traffic.

In general, eBPF can be used for implementing custom traffic management and monitoring solutions in Linux. By attaching eBPF programs to various points in the kernel's networking stack, you can gain a high level of control over how traffic is processed and handled. This can be useful in various scenarios, such as optimizing network performance, improving security, or gaining insight into network traffic patterns.

In this chapter, we will implement a simple **port redirector** using two eBPF programs, one at the ingress and the other at the egress of the networking stack. The port redirector will punt the incoming traffic meant for one port to another port on the server. In this example, a Linux server will have an HTTP server listening on port 8081. However, the port advertised to the external world will be 8080. When an HTTP client sends an HTTP request to port 8080, the **ingress** eBPF program will change the destination port in the TCP header of the request packet from 8080 to 8081. The modified packet with the updated port is then handed over to the networking stack for further processing. After the HTTP server has processed the packet and sent a response, the **egress** eBPF program will change the source port of the response packet from 8081 to 8080. As a result, the HTTP client is completely unaware of the HTTP request being served by a different port on the Linux server.

User Space Program

```
52 let intf = "eth0";
53
54 let _ = tc::qdisc_add_clsact(&intf);
55 let mut program: &mut SchedClassifier =
56         bpf.program_mut("tc_ingress").unwrap()
```

```
            .try_into()?;
57 program.load()?;
58 program
59     .attach(&intf, TcAttachType::Ingress)?;
60
61 program = bpf.program_mut("tc_egress").unwrap()
                .try_into()?;
62 program.load()?;
63 program
64    .attach(&intf, TcAttachType::Egress)?;
```

- Line 54: Add a traffic control action to the interface whose traffic needs to be port redirected.

- Lines 55 - 59: Load and attach the ingress eBPF program.

- Lines 61 - 64: Load and attach the egress eBPF program.

Ingress eBPF Program

```
19 const HTTP_ADV_PORT: u16 = 8080;
20 const HTTP_ACT_PORT: u16 = 8081;
21
22 const ETH_P_IP: u16 = 0x0800;
23 const ETH_HDR_LEN: usize = mem::size_of::<ethhdr>();
24 const IP_HDR_LEN: usize = mem::size_of::<iphdr>();
25 const TCP_PROTOCOL: u8 = 0x06;
26 const TCP_SRC_PORT_OFFSET: usize =
27     ETH_HDR_LEN + IP_HDR_LEN;
28 const TCP_DST_PORT_OFFSET: usize =
29     ETH_HDR_LEN + IP_HDR_LEN + 2;
30 const TCP_CHECKSUM_OFFSET: usize =
31     ETH_HDR_LEN + IP_HDR_LEN + 16;
```

```
32
33 #[classifier(name="tc_ingress")]
34 pub fn tc_ingress(ctx: TcContext) -> i32 {
35   match try_tc_ingress(ctx) {
36     Ok(ret) => ret,
37     Err(ret) => ret,
38   }
39 }
40
41 fn try_tc_ingress(mut ctx: TcContext)
             -> Result<i32, i32> {
42
43   let eth_proto = u16::from_be(
44     ctx.load(offset_of!(ethhdr, h_proto))
           .map_err(|_| TC_ACT_PIPE)?,
46   );
47   if eth_proto != ETH_P_IP {
48     return Ok(TC_ACT_PIPE);
49   }
50
51   let protocol = u8::from_be(
52     ctx.load(ETH_HDR_LEN + offset_of!(iphdr,
                                 protocol))
           .map_err(|_| TC_ACT_PIPE)?,
54   );
55
56   if protocol != TCP_PROTOCOL {
57     return Ok(TC_ACT_PIPE);
58   }
59
60   let dst_port = u16::from_be(
61     ctx.load(TCP_DST_PORT_OFFSET)
           .map_err(|_| TC_ACT_PIPE)?,
63   );
64
```

```
65    if dst_port != HTTP_ADV_PORT {
66      return Ok(TC_ACT_PIPE);
67    }
68
69    ctx.l4_csum_replace(TCP_CHECKSUM_OFFSET,
70      HTTP_ADV_PORT.to_be() as u64,
71      HTTP_ACT_PORT.to_be() as u64, 2)
72      .map_err(|_| TC_ACT_PIPE)?;
73
74    ctx.store(TCP_DST_PORT_OFFSET,
            &HTTP_ACT_PORT.to_be(), 0)
75      .map_err(|_| TC_ACT_PIPE)?;
76
77    info!(&ctx, "Redirected TCP traffic from " +
            "{} to port {}",
78      HTTP_ADV_PORT, HTTP_ACT_PORT);
79
80    Ok(TC_ACT_PIPE)
81 }
```

- Line 19: Port advertised to external clients as the HTTP port.

- Line 20: Port to which the ingress eBPF program redirects the HTTP traffic.

- Lines 22 - 31: Constants that define the protocol numbers, packet header lengths, and offsets.

- Lines 33 - 39: The ingress eBPF classifier program. The context for the eBPF classifier program is a sk_buff.

- Lines 43 - 67: Check if the network packet is a TCP packet with the source port set to HTTP_ADV_PORT (8080). If not, the eBPF program completes with a return value of

TC_ACT_PIPE, which indicates that the packet can be processed further by any other ingress classifier programs and filters.

- Lines 69 - 78: Change the destination port of the TCP packet to HTTP_ACT_PORT (8081). In addition, the TCP checksum is updated to match the new destination port.

- Line 80: The eBPF program returns with TC_ACT_PIPE, allowing the packet to be processed further on the ingress path.

Egress eBPF Program

```
82
83 #[classifier(name="tc_egress")]
84 pub fn tc_egress(ctx: TcContext) -> i32 {
85   match try_tc_egress(ctx) {
86       Ok(ret) => ret,
87       Err(ret) => ret,
88   }
89 }
90
91 fn try_tc_egress(mut ctx: TcContext) -> Result<i32,
   i32> {
92
93   let eth_proto = u16::from_be(
94     ctx.load(offset_of!(ethhdr, h_proto))
95         .map_err(|_| TC_ACT_PIPE)?,
96   );
97   if eth_proto != ETH_P_IP {
98     return Ok(TC_ACT_PIPE);
99   }
100
```

```
101    let protocol = u8::from_be(
102      ctx.load(ETH_HDR_LEN + offset_of!(iphdr,
    protocol))
103         .map_err(|_| TC_ACT_PIPE)?,
104    );
105
106    if protocol != TCP_PROTOCOL {
107      return Ok(TC_ACT_PIPE);
108    }
109
110    let src_port = u16::from_be(
111      ctx.load(TCP_SRC_PORT_OFFSET)
112         .map_err(|_| TC_ACT_PIPE)?,
113    );
114
115    if src_port != HTTP_ACT_PORT {
116      return Ok(TC_ACT_PIPE);
117    }
118
119    ctx.l4_csum_replace(TCP_CHECKSUM_OFFSET,
120      HTTP_ACT_PORT.to_be() as u64,
121      HTTP_ADV_PORT.to_be() as u64, 2)
122      .map_err(|_| TC_ACT_PIPE)?;
123
124
125    ctx.store(TCP_SRC_PORT_OFFSET, &HTTP_ADV_PORT.
    to_be(), 0)
126      .map_err(|_| TC_ACT_PIPE)?;
127
128    info!(&ctx, "Changed the source port from {} to
    port {}",
129      HTTP_ACT_PORT, HTTP_ADV_PORT);
130
131    Ok(TC_ACT_PIPE)
132 }
```

- Lines 83 - 89: The egress eBPF classifier program. The context for the eBPF classifier program is a sk_buff.

- Lines 93 - 117: Check if the network packet is a TCP packet with the destination port set to HTTP_ACT_PORT (8081). If not, the eBPF program completes with a return value of TC_ACT_PIPE, which indicates that the packet can be processed further by any other egress classifier programs and filters.

- Lines 119 - 126: Change the source port of the TCP packet to HTTP_ADV_PORT (8080). In addition, the TCP checksum is updated to match the updated source port.

- Line 131: The eBPF program returns with TC_ACT_PIPE, allowing the packet to be processed further on the egress path.

Test

With the above eBPF programs running, you can run a python HTTP server on the Linux box using the command.

```
python3 -m http.server 8081
```

With the HTTP server running on port 8081, you should be able to successfully send an HTTP request using curl to the server at port 8080.

→

```
curl -I http://<hostname>:8080

HTTP/1.0 200 OK
Server: SimpleHTTP/0.6 Python/3.8.10
Date: Wed, 21 Dec 2022 02:41:20 GMT
Content-type: text/html; charset=utf-8
Content-Length: 884
```

Program Array

As mentioned earlier, the size of an eBPF program is restricted to a million instructions to limit the problem space of the eBPF verifier. With this restriction, implementing a non-trivial kernel functionality using eBPF requires decomposing the functionality into multiple eBPF programs. References to the multiple eBPF programs can be stored in a Program Array Map, and the control can then flow from one eBPF program to another using the **bpf_tail_call** API call. In this book's final chapter, we will demonstrate this functionality by decomposing the Socket Filter Program into multiple eBPF programs.

The single eBPF program will be decomposed into four separate eBPF programs. Three eBPF programs will be stored in an eBPF Program Array Map. The top-level eBPF program will use the **sk_buff** to determine the L4 protocol. Depending on the protocol type, the control will be passed to a different eBPF program using the Program Array Map to increment the packet counter.

Userspace program

```
51 let mut counters: HashMap<_, u8, u32> =
52   HashMap::try_from(bpf.map_mut("COUNTERS")?)?;
53 let mut prog_array = ProgramArray::try_from(
54   bpf.map_mut("JUMP_TABLE")?,
55 )?;
56
57 let client = unsafe {
58   libc::socket(
59       libc::AF_PACKET,
60       libc::SOCK_RAW,
61       ETH_P_ALL.to_be() as i32,
62   )
63 };
64 let prog: &mut SocketFilter = bpf
65   .program_mut("prg_arr_map")
66   .unwrap()
67   .try_into()?;
68 prog.load()?;
69 prog.attach(client.as_raw_fd())?;
70
71 let tcp_prog: &mut SocketFilter = bpf
72   .program_mut("process_tcp")
73   .unwrap()
74   .try_into()?;
75 tcp_prog.load()?;
76 prog_array.set(TCP_PROG_IDX, tcp_prog, 0)?;
77
78 let udp_prog: &mut SocketFilter = bpf
79   .program_mut("process_udp")
80   .unwrap()
81   .try_into()?;
82 udp_prog.load()?;
83 prog_array.set(UDP_PROG_IDX, udp_prog, 0)?;
84
85 let icmp_prog: &mut SocketFilter = bpf
```

```
86    .program_mut("process_icmp")
87    .unwrap()
88    .try_into()?;
89 icmp_prog.load()?;
90 prog_array.set(ICMP_PROG_IDX, icmp_prog, 0)?;
```

- Lines 53 - 55: Declare a Program Array Map to hold three eBPF programs.

- Lines 64 - 68: Load the main eBPF program.

- Line 69: Attach the main eBPF program to the raw socket.

- Lines 71 - 75: Load the eBPF program to increment the counter for TCP packets.

- Line 76: Add the program to the program array map with TCP_PROG_IDX (integer value of 0) key.

- Lines 78 - 82: Load the eBPF program to increment the counter for UDP packets.

- Line 83: Add the program to the program array map with UDP_PROG_IDX (integer value of 1) key.

- Lines 85 - 89: Load the eBPF program that will increment the counter for ICMP packets.

- Line 90: Add the program to the program array map with ICMP_PROG_IDX (integer value of 2) key.

eBPF program

```
24 #[map(name = "COUNTERS")]
25 static mut COUNTERS: HashMap<u8, u32> =
```

```
26    HashMap::<u8, u32>::with_max_entries(3, 0);
27
28 #[map(name = "JUMP_TABLE")]
29 static mut JUMP_TABLE: ProgramArray =
30    ProgramArray::with_max_entries(3, 0);
31
32 fn increment_counter(proto: u8) {
33    let mut counter =
34        unsafe { COUNTERS.get(&proto).unwrap_or(&0) };
35    let new_count = *counter + 1;
36    unsafe {
37        COUNTERS.insert(&proto, &new_count, 0).unwrap()
38    };
39 }
40
41 #[socket_filter(name = "process_icmp")]
42 pub fn process_icmp(_ctx: SkBuffContext) -> i64 {
43    increment_counter(ICMP_PROTO);
44    return 0;
45 }
46
47 #[socket_filter(name = "process_tcp")]
48 pub fn process_tcp(_ctx: SkBuffContext) -> i64 {
49    increment_counter(TCP_PROTO);
50    return 0;
51 }
52
53 #[socket_filter(name = "process_udp")]
54 pub fn process_udp(_ctx: SkBuffContext) -> i64 {
55    increment_counter(UDP_PROTO);
56    return 0;
57 }
58
59 #[socket_filter(name = "prg_arr_map")]
60 pub fn prg_arr_map(_ctx: SkBuffContext) -> i64 {
```

```
61    let eth_proto = u16::from_be(
62      _ctx.load(offset_of!(ethhdr, h_proto))
63          .unwrap(),
64    );
65    let ip_proto = _ctx
66      .load::<u8>(
67          ETH_HDR_LEN + offset_of!(iphdr, protocol),
68      )
69      .unwrap();
70
71    if eth_proto != IP_PROTO {
72      return 0;
73    }
74
75    match ip_proto {
76      TCP_PROTO => unsafe {
77          JUMP_TABLE.tail_call(&_ctx, TCP_PROG_IDX);
78      },
79      ICMP_PROTO => unsafe {
80          JUMP_TABLE.tail_call(&_ctx, ICMP_PROG_IDX);
81      },
82      UDP_PROTO => unsafe {
83          JUMP_TABLE.tail_call(&_ctx, UDP_PROG_IDX);
84      },
85      _ => {}
86    }
87
88    return 0;
89 }
```

- Lines 28 - 30: Define a program array map to hold the three eBPF programs.

- Lines 32 - 39: Define a function to increment the packet

107

counter. All three eBPF programs will share this function.

- Lines 41 - 45: eBPF program to increment the packet count for ICMP packets.

- Lines 47 - 51: eBPF program to increment the packet count for TCP packets.

- Lines 53 - 57: eBPF program to increment the packet count for UDP packets.

- Line 59: Define the main eBPF program that will be executed as the packet filter.

- Lines 75 - 86: Depending on the packet type, jump to the appropriate eBPF program to increment the counter.